WITHDRAWN

EAST OF HATTERAS

EAST OF HATTERAS

SELECTED POEMS

By

ROBERT RENTOUL REED, JR.

THE CHRISTOPHER PUBLISHING HOUSE
NORTH QUINCY, MASSACHUSETTS
02171

PRINTED IN

THE UNITED STATES OF AMERICA

To Judy, Wendy
and Christine

TABLE OF CONTENTS

EAST OF HATTERAS

ON LOOKING BACK

There was no death that I recall
When I was young and skies were bright;
Then every tot, however small,
Kept in his heart an angel's light.

Each garden square then teemed with life;
In every nest ten birds were born:
There seemed to be no place for strife
Or thoughts of death in that bright morn.

If death was there, it lurked unseen
At garden wall, in pond and fold:
So near to God, I saw the bean
Sprout sunward like a world of gold.

The child sees not the withered stalk
Or sparrow fallen from the air;
On dark, unfriended shores he'll walk
And see bright angels everywhere.

THE YOUNG WHO'VE DIED

At night I've heard them cry for peace
    And for the Great Down-Under:
Sometimes as soft as doves they'll cry,
    Sometimes in peals of thunder.

A few may be the Grecian dead
    Unburied on the plain,
But others are the young who've died
    And have come back again.

Some undone task, I think, remains
    To each who has died young:
The priest read "Dust to dust," but left
    God's requiem unsung.

From setting suns they come at night;
    They sleep in dawn-lit streams:
Meantime, to long-abandoned doors
    They lead us in our dreams.

LOST REALM

How gone? And whither? A moment's call has stayed
The vital clock which ticked her happy hours
Of love and childhood when she sang and played
Among the hedge-rows and her garden flowers.
No longer do her happy strains arise
Across the terrace to her mother's ears,
But now the garden hears the threnodies
Of wintry-wind for desolate long years.
Sometimes a cold moon scales the eastern flight
And, drifting through the jeweled skies above,
Unveils the garden to the pausing night,
Enthralled to hear a melody of love:
    A little child with phantom step surveys
    Her ruined realm of not forgotten days.

THE SHEPHERD OF UR

The Babylonian, on some ancient night,
Stirred from his sleep and, hardly knowing why,
Could sleep no more; but, lying half in fright,
He searched the mystery of his heathen sky.
He gazed and gazed, remembering from his youth
His gray-haired sire, who left the tale untold—
The mystery of space and time and truth,
The light of stars ten thousand centuries old!
Immeasurable! The shepherd searched, and saw
No answer there in that unfathomed stream
Of silent stars; but still he gazed in awe,
And could not sleep . . . half-hearing, as in dream,
        The old Euphrates, muttering coded rhyme,
        Speak of the "Bridegroom" of prenatal time.

NANTUCKET

Nantucket slept, benumbed by summer fog,
Before the morning sun had drawn the veil
Of mid-night dew from moor and town and dale,
From drowsing shore or sleeping inland-bog.
Soon, songs of meadow-larks, the voice of dawn,
Rose out the mists, dispelled the still of night;
More swiftly now the eastern bands of light
Shot forth; and the protracted dark slid on.
Slow horse-hooves clanked upon the cobbled street,
And fishing-smacks went chugging through the bay
Beneath the mists which late refused the day,
While, on the shore, the far-off ocean's beat
    Was drumming welcome to the vibrant sun
    Through broken bars, by elf or midnight spun.

THE GYPSY'S SONG

I heard her song—she sang upon a shore
Where mirthful waters mingle with the strain
Of slumbering elms—then, sweeping backward, pour
Like sullen mist upon the laughing main.
O laugh, wild waters! forests, ever weep!
The one is free; the one, eternal-bound.
O laugh, bright waters! while the forests sleep
In captive woe, by slumbrous ages crowned!
I heard her song; the waves and forest heard,
As lithe she stole along the silver sands
And gaily sang the songs that freedom stirred—
Light-hearted echoes of a thousand lands!
    Gay child of Freedom, daughter of the sea,
    Yours is the world—wild elms encompass me.

BLUE MOUNTAINS

I hardly know from where I came, nor why;
Perhaps by chance I breathe this mortal air;
There seems no reason, yet I would not die
Lest death give reason to my being here.
I would not die; and yet sometimes I dream
Of cold blue mountains and a frosty soil;
And, when most weary, those blue mountains seem
A promised refuge from relentless toil.
Some day, perhaps, I must depart and go;
Yet I should never call such going "death,"
No more than when the long-awaited snow
Shuts out the autumn and its weary breath.
    Dark entails dawnlight; and I've dreamt from
        birth
    Of cold blue mountains and a frozen earth.

SPRING OF TOMORROW

Somewhere, some day, this truth must surely be—
Throughout our land some happy thrush shall sing
A song unknown, which, pouring sea to sea,
Shall wake the trumpets of a deathless Spring.
All things shall hear this awesome harmony,
City and tower—the hills, the woods, the shore;
And hearts, forgetful of stark Winter's sting,
Shall bloom in beauties never known before.
And there shall be an angel's counterpart,
A spiritual Spring accented from Above,
Uniting nations, heart to common heart,
In sworn allegiance, unforgiving love.
    If such can be, men dwarfed with hate and strife
    Shall stand amazed—shocked by the warmth of
    Life!

FIRESIDE

The hearth tonight sheds an untempered glow;
Its dancing shadows pitch and laugh and toss
Along the walls, as if they did not know
That you were dead, that I should mourn your loss.
I cannot weep; the gay philosophy
Of these mute shadows steals each anxious tear;
They laugh and laugh, unchanged and endlessly,
Forever young, each phantom buccaneer.
Forever young. . . . Life's story is retold:
I'll live to wither on the rack of Time;
But you shall sit here, ever as of old,
Unchanged and lovely—in perpetual rhyme
    With laughing shadows and unchanging truth,
    Prince of that world, where nothing can blunt
       youth.

TO MY BROTHER JACK

(A contradictory ten-year-old rascal)

You are an impish little elf
With no regard but for yourself.
You think the world was made for you
And nought is mischief that you do.
You're never wrong, but always right;
Upbraidings you regard with spite;
No one can prompt you or advise
For older wisdoms you despise.
All social laws, conventions meet
Defiance in your stamping feet;
While God help those whose ways transgress
On your despotic stubbornness!

But, brother, hearken to my word;
Perhaps you'll profit, once you've heard:
To all Creation's laws, you're friction—
In fact, an outright contradiction.
What hope is there if you disdain
Paternal warnings, shrewd but plain?
What hope is there if you deride
A mother's caution, long defied?
O there is hope, my little scout;

You merely turn your wrong side out;
But look within and you will find
A wiser self therein confined:
May it grow ripe, and you will learn
That charity must serve its turn.
The heart can be a sun-bright place
When tiger and the Lamb embrace.

PLAYMATES

O listen, stranger, to their laughter:
Does it matter what comes after?
    Bubbling laughter, bubbling joy,
    Little children, girl and boy,
    Nearer God than we can be,
    Havened by Infinity!
    Blind to sorrow, bubbling mirth,
    Loving all things of the Earth,
    Loving bird and sun and flower,
    Loving every woodland hour—
Theirs is more than gold can buy,
Laughing heart and laughing sky!
    Merrily their footsteps pass,
    Tiny footsteps through the grass,
    Merrily, each girl and boy—
    Thoughtless yet of hearts that hate,
    Thoughtless of the bolt and gate.
O listen, stranger, to their laughter:
Does it matter what comes after?

YOUTH EVERLASTING

I've watched the sun sink down an April sky
And, like a fireball, smoulder on the west,
Seen virgin-red fade to the darkening dye
Of scented night, on Spring's clear-bubbling breast:
    Rich-throated, then, was heard the nightingale
    In fertile sorrow, from an upland vale.

I too have seen the withered winter sun
Trek out his day, sigh forth his ghostly light
On naked hills, in stark oblivion,
And silent sink before devouring night.
    Gaunt and ill-famed: then, from a shivering dell,
    A lonesome owl sounded forth his knell!

A hideous dark! At once I dreamt again
Of April suns . . . of Spring's rich-fading day;
Thus dreaming, yearned, among life-loving men,
That I might pass so youthfully away:
    That I might die, and dying proud and young,
    Wake in a glade where nightingales have sung.

REQUEST IN JULY

Grant me the hills where the gnarled wind plays
    Its woodstruck melody,
And the lonesome brook fills summer days
    In unpent ecstasy;
Where oak and the ash spread a jagged shade
    Beneath the noonday heat,
And the latticed moonlight haunts each glade
    Prowling on cat-like feet.

I've dreamt of a shack beside the brook
    Where untampered trout await,
So lend me a rod, and a gun, and a book—
    A pipe to meditate.
What's more, I'll find a God out there
    To saintly creeds unvowed:
While the wind up-blows his golden hair,
    He sharpens a thunder-cloud.

AFTERGLOW

The love that's long remembered
    Is man's astonished first;
It loosens the soul from bondage,
    From dark and fretful thirst.

Inside our garden at noonday,
    O loved one, then full white,
Each kiss sped the wing of eagles,
    But left a rosebud's blight.

The laughter that quivered to silence
    On hills beyond the sun—
Remember the laughter, my darling;
    Ask not why love is done.

When, tired, I've reached Life's deltas,
    Where currents back and flow,
I'll dream of eagles soaring
    On mountains filled with snow;

I'll dream of untrod glaciers
    From which the wind-torn spray
Leaps, sun-bright, like an arrow
    Across the roof of day.

END OF TWO TRAILS

"What lurks," one asked, "beyond that bend?
    What storm or tempests blow?"
He sought, instead, the stalwart shade
    Of elm and mistletoe.

But Death, who peers in every bush,
    Will some day spy him out,
And he who feared to round the bend
    Prompts then no trumpet's shout.

His pride is that he is head clerk—
    Sells lace and gloves, full time;
But there are other men more brave
    Who found new hills to climb.

They had no fear to round the bend
    Or hack out paths untrod:
And now above each thunderhead
    They catch a glimpse of God.

A CHRISTMAS INCIDENT

Indeed, there was a Christmas day
    Before, on Earth, Christ stepped:
Then, in a blue and sun-girt land
    A child's first tear was wept—

A tear that made a rainbow shine
    For miles and miles on end—
As she beheld the gift he'd brought
    Who boasted of no friend.

The recluse "humphed" and marked her tears;
    He scowled and doffed his cap:
"That doll," he said, "cost not a cent
    But rags I'd have to scrap."

Dark though his words, at heart she felt
    Warmth and relief and thrill:
That night, she dreamt the farthest star
    Spoke from her windowsill.

TO A BEREAVED MATRON

You merely said he'd passed away,
No more was said—I understood
That when the sun sinks from the day
There is no laughter in the wood.
No laughter, then, but soon the dawn
Must break again, its glow impart
The laughter from the day that's gone,
New courage vibrant in each heart.
Or has he died, whose life is read
In minds made brave, in hearts that hold
Bright cheer from him? Can one be dead
When shrined in hearts, a thousandfold?

VANITAS ARROGANTIAE

Proud-eyed Ambition kindles meager men,
And they have clambered upward to the stars
In mad ascent, not glancing back again
Till they have viewed the citadels of Mars.
Then, dazed with folly of his sated mind,
Each spurns the steps by which he did ascend
And leers contempt on those he left behind,
Disdains them all, and calls no man his friend.
Be not too proud, nor scorn your brother's lot;
Sometimes the eaglet soars on morning wing
To rest at noon, shorn by the hunter's shot,
A vulgar offering to the woodland Spring.
    Some hand, unmarked, curbs folly in its pride,
    And no man lives but keeps a fool inside.

TAONGI

The laughing wave, the island, that is all
There ever was, and there shall never be
Another thing except the bird's sharp call
That floats so idly on this tropic sea.
Sometimes at morn it is a lonely thing
To hear a gull cry from a neighboring dune,
To watch him soar, then drift on sun-bright wing
To secrets hid within a far lagoon.
Then, walled by silence, one can only hear
Sea-music swooning on the pebbled shore,
And start at death and wish Ulysses near,
Who, through resolve, thought of the breakers' roar
    On far-off Ithaca; while close at hand
        The lotus bloomed, and dreamful was the land.

A RIDGE TO CROSS

I sometimes fear my heart is growing old,
As in September dreamful boys are sad,
Recalling how in April glades, sun-gold,
The wood thrush sang, its accents ever glad.
Thus, in the autumn, pensive youngsters dream
Of merry haunts far from their school-room door;
And, thinking back, a summer's day will seem
A dance of light upon a seaside shore.
Not fate or years have dulled such dreaming's power:
When tired at heart, I hear my boyhood's thrush
And vision meadows bright and gaudy flower
And rainbows painted by an angel's brush.
    I would go back; but men, once grown, are vowed
    To gods who watch them from a thunder-cloud.

THE FLEDGLING

We cannot ask them how it was to die:
We are but fledglings unbaptized by Death
And know but Earth and the blue dome of sky:
We cannot ask them of that crucial breath,
For they, far speeding, left us prisoners here,
Encircled by the dark side of the moon.
One autumn at the death-bed of one dear
When I had doubts, as at a Druid's rune,
And would deny that souls could be reborn
Or substance had, more than the Earth's own dark,
I searched the dying face, blind and flesh-worn,
And thought of lilacs and the sky-borne lark
    And spires, dawn-bright. I thought of angels who,
    Unseen, have walked through flame-gold Xanadu.

AMONG THE MOUNTAINS

I know a place where men can't even spell
Their name in ink, nor do they understand
One printed word. Indeed, they vaguely tell
No truth exists beyond their mountain-land.
They do not know the markets of Mankind,
The lore of Plato or old Shylock's greed;
They do not know the worth of Dante's mind;
Theirs is the soil; theirs is a coarser creed.
Call them uncouth; and yet they are most wise;
They know the seasons and the seasons' yield;
Theirs is the knowledge and the enterprise
Of calloused hand and golden-studded field.
    But, most of all, they shelter in their sod
    The timeless wisdom of their native God.

EARTH SONG

Not in old forests, nor by winter streams
Of rivers mumbling with the frost of Time,
Not in the ancient catacombs of dreams,
Nor by the sea, nor in an august clime—
In none of these, but here among the hills,
Lost to the world, known only to the skies,
Where virgin winds sport with the daffodils,
Where all is young, and nothing ever dies:
Rich solitudes! These are the founts, the birth,
Of song first spoken in the long ago;
Eternally, the wind-struck bards of Earth
Played on and on. . . . Perhaps the heavens know
       What harp speaks truth as does the wind-
            blown flower
       Or bird that sings, rain-bright from April
            shower.

THE PARTHENON

How mighty yet! Mid age-worn dust she stands,
Too proud to yield, while Time treads up and down,
Completing bit by bit with pilfering hands
The slow destruction of her marbled gown.
Not Turk nor foe could stem her sceptered heart;
Her chambers cloven, still she stands serene,
Forbidding ruin, cleaving storm apart,
A broken empress—but proud-hearted queen!
Once beauteous, her stricken beauty holds
Some mightier strength within its hallowed space
Of emptiness, girt by those pillared molds,
Those Doric columns—that stupendous grace!
    Above her now, no roof but watching sky;
    About her feet the scattered centuries lie.

PILGRIM AT EVE

There is a beach thrice girt with rocks around;
And here at dusk, late from some daily chore—
Descending slow—I've heard the mystic sound
That ocean waters make against the shore.
Remote, alone, I've stood before the wave
As at an altar, gaining secret birth,
And heard old music sounding in a cave—
The noise of waters twice as old as Earth.
I've heard old music such as Pan awoke
When first he played in far Sicilian clime—
Ancestral, full, as though gold concerts broke
On cavern walls in tongues of olden time—
    Among them Sappho's, siren of the deep,
    Who lulls the burning sunset seas to sleep.

THE IDEALIST

I crowned her with a crown of gold,
    Red rose for raven hair,
And robed her in a robe of white
    With frill of whitest fur.

I carved for her a marble throne,
    Made her a sceptered rod,
Placed her above all other things—
    Save one almighty God.

Her palace now in crystal stone
    Looks down the pillared sky;
The gate is barred—I little thought
    How skilled a dunce was I!

CHIMES AT NOON

(Written in Southern California)

The mission bells toll out the mid of day,
Resounding fragments of old Spanish lay;
Remote, yet full, each note leaps forth its gong,
Then wayward scurries in melodious song;
Echoes, reechoed from the mountains, blend
With fresher notes that richer fullness lend—
And on the village by the palm-fringed sea
There hangs, dream-like, an opal canopy.

Thus sweet, enchanted melodies in tune
Swell out the rhythm of the pausing noon,
And softly fall upon the fragrant shore
In lingering echo to the cottage door.
How sweet the rhythm, sweeter yet the pause
The noonday hour from our labor draws:
A book is dropped; a housewife's art foregone;
The gardener's hoe from rasping toil withdrawn.
All thoughts embraced, this ebb of day spellbound
In minstrel fullness and enchanted sound:
Hushed is the wind, locked in a seaside cave,
Entranced the motion of the traveled wave;
While, by the sea, the razored palm-tree stands
In breathless gust above the shadowed sands.

O transient moment, transitory tune
That breaks the morning and the afternoon!
Far flown the bells; but now in lingering strain
Their bridled motion pours the slow refrain:
Now slower . . . fainter . . . ever more remote
Till fades the echo of the last-born note,
And trembles on the bosom of the sea,
Engulfed in silence and immensity.

TROPIC FRAGMENT

The night is different here: a lasting calm
Engulfs the shore, enfolds the starlit wave,
And fills with rustling of some sleepless palm
The purple silence of the tropic cave.
Thus all is night upon this southern shore,
A magic dark, where faery-folk embalm
Both earth and sea in an expectant grave,
Till nothing stirs, and Time forgets his chore,
And life is lost to fancy evermore.

It is the hour: close by the circling stream
Of breathless waters, moves the tropic moon;
Thence, slow ascending, sheds her golden beam
Till all the sea stirs in a rippled swoon.
Hence kingdoms cease, and beings cease to be;
Though none knows why, all human task is dream;
Tomorrow sleeps upon a far lagoon
As Death has slept; meantime the moonstruck sea
Flames like a fragment of Eternity.

CHILDREN OF THE SEA

I

Night on night I've heard the Ocean, heard
    each earthen god reviled—
Heard the Ocean's dreaded voice, where I
    knelt once as a child.

Having heard, I've guessed the meaning—
    saints of darkness, shelter me!
Mountains are her great god-children; nothing
    was before the Sea.

First she cried on deep-delved altars, now her
    passions are unbound,
Rising to the stars in anger, chiding with
    a hallowed sound.

Though she chide, I cannot scorn her;
    else I scorn my primal birth,
Hidden somewhere down the ages, on
    the borders of the Earth.

Courage, brother! turn, nor answer—we, the
    twin-born of the Sea—
We must fly both town and tavern, marks of our
    mortality.

II

Grime-faced alleys fall behind us, farther
    fades the city-wall;
Music mingles, and we answer; far ahead the
    waters call.

Hearken how each hoofbeat clatters, like a
    tempo to the Sea;
Spur to spur, we gallop onward—she is calling
    you and me.

Louder, louder comes her voice—deeper beats
    the surf below:
Madly is the dark Sea calling for her
    children long ago—

Calling like some weeping mother who has seen
    her children sin,
Calling to us to attend her, to attend
    her plaintive din.

We have come; now all around us, mid the
    rocks and cliffs and caves,
Spread the Ocean's silken tresses, echo all
    her weeping waves.

Now she points to starlit summits, tossing on
    the night above;
Now she dips amid the caverns, pouring forth
    new songs of love.

Moonless is the dark about us, purple is
    the Ocean's breast,
Purple as the wines in autumn, foaming
    yet with whitened crest.

Skyward rising, now she mocks us, chiding
    lest we disobey;
Softer, softer, falls her voice as the white
    surf rolls away.

III

Ages here were born in sorrow; we have
    washed from Wisdom's stream:
We must tell the Sea, our Mother, that
    our sin was but a dream.

We must tell her our repentance: though
    we've sat at Folly's board,
Servitude must be redemption; Life was
    but a hostile lord.

Wines of folly and of blindness, wines we
    drank in earliest youth,
Giddier far than wines of Assur, numbed
    our eyes to right and truth.

Hark, she mocks in stern forgiveness: warmly
    now her purple wave
Rises shoreward to caress us, opens forth
    its yawning grave.

Darkly gleam the stars above us, urging,
    in their silent way,
Words forgotten in the centuries, bidding
    that we must obey.

Hush, the wind blows softly by us, blowing
    voices of the dead,
Of the wise men and the poets whom the
    sinful ages bred.

Hearken, softly do they tell us that our
    Mother is the Sea;
That the cup of God once broken, she
    commands, "Come back to me."

Priests who sinned have gone before us; and
    the darkness stretches far,
Touching on the walls of Heaven, brightened by
    the farthest star.

We who've strutted like young godlings, we
    must seek death-mocking wine
In the oneness of forgiveness, from
    the breasts of our Divine;

Fear not, therefore, our first Mother mindful of
    the sin she bore:
Warmly shall her wave enfold us, warmly,
    warmly, evermore!

REUNION

When torn at heart, in dreams I find
A place that's strange to know:
A Gothic square where poppies bloom
And mourners nod, then go.

Quite often, at the village pump,
A mourner waits apart—
And, as we meet, her upturned eyes
Reach to the inner heart.

I'm sure that she has lost me too,
For sometimes, as we roam
Among the maze of Gothic streets,
She talks to me of home.

But where our home is, angels know;
Perhaps some outlaw's cave
Foreknew our love, not yet fulfilled
In dreams beyond the grave.

APRIL DEATH

When April's day was strong and lustful,
    I would watch the midday sun;
I would walk in lusty meadows,
    Counting flowers one by one.

But April's day is grown much older,
    And the passions of my youth
Walk no more in magic meadows—
    I stand upon the hill of Truth.

Let April fade, I will not tremble;
    But down into the valley go,
Where strong men reap September's harvest
    Against the autumn and the snow.

DEPARTURE

"My boots hang by the old corral,
My saddle is in the shed—
Tomorrow morn I'll saddle up
Before the dawn is red."

The dawn broke red, then palely moved
Across the desert sands:
A horseman climbed the westward ridge
That borders the mountain-lands.

No one knows where that rider went
When he left the old corral;
The law of the desert was never to ask,
But only "Good luck, old pal!"

THE SECOND CALL

"Look in thy heart, and write"—but there I find
No Stella's image and her saint-like gaze,
Which tuned the chords of Philip Sidney's mind
To gain from England yet-untarnished praise.
There is no angel-maiden in my heart
To mold in me the soul that's perfect made,
That speaks the soldier in the poet's art
And poet-courtier under cannonade.
Once in my heart a child did strum the lute,
But he is dead, and now no maiden sings;
Yet there is solace in a heart that's mute
As in dark quarries where will bloom no springs:
 Thus Milton found that wisdom clearest shone
 From out a heart grown passionless as stone.

THE PHANTOM'S CRY

I can't recall on what dark shoal of fame
The gods turned back; my doom has been to roam
The world's wide orb, and seek and find a home
Beyond the sea-mark of the world's acclaim.
Both sought and seeking, I've lived centuries through,
And I am nothing but a spirit tossed
On mist-gold seas, still searching and still lost;
From crag and cliff, the fatal Sirens woo.
What am I? Well, my birth was Marathon;
I molded Venus with my gifted hands,
The thigh and breast that Nature understands,
And carved the frieze about the Parthenon.
    By Keats perhaps, my art has been restored:
    I quicken mostly when I'm most ignored.

FALLEN SOLDIER, YEARS AFTERWARDS

I came not here in triumph: few men heed
My nameless stone, and no wreath rims my brow;
And, being dead, I ask no deference now,
For bird and fox have taught a second creed.
When I had lain in this slight grave of mine
One winter long, sun-dark as tombs can be,
I woke and heard a bird-sung rhapsody,
Though muffled by dead needles of the pine.
Till then I had not understood bird-song:
But now I know that I, with bird and fox,
Am one with roots and with untended clocks,
And each with ocean sand. Thus, before long,
    You may see a rose float by on a stream
    And so mark me, who of dark oceans dream.

TWO AUTUMNS

Aloof on hills more barren than
    The stark and cold November,
Not Aeschylus himself has told
    Quite all the dead remember.

For text he chose that ancient theme
    The dead condone no ill,
And showed how Agamemnon chafed
    Entombed in his great hill.

Staunch as the tomb, a mandate came,
    And reckless was the king:
Doom paid for doom, and on his son
    Set loose the Fury's wing.

The vengeful dead are prudent now
    And cautious, who recall
The price of Clytemnestra's doom
    Watched by the haunted wall.

At thoughts, I think, of scarlet leaves
    And gaunt Orestes' woe,
They startle; and their vengeance breaks
    Dreamless in shrouds of snow.

BRIGHTER SPEAK

Unshared the cup though, hand in hand,
　　They spent the stormy time,
Defiant of the gods who quelled
　　Bright ardor at its prime.

The months and years have passed since then;
　　Cold gleams the fresh white snow;
Tonight the thought of his hand's touch
　　Has set her heart aglow.

John Donne, I think, was amply wise:
　　Though seas and mountain peak
Keep man from girl and banish sight,
　　Soul unto soul will speak;

And brighter speak beyond the grave.
　　For, there, no right or wrong,
No code among the Pleiades,
　　Dissuades one's soul from song.

FALSTAFF AND THE PRINCE

No king "hath kill'd" your heart, Sir John;
Dame Quickly's words were your most bold-faced lie.
Only we, the flesh, have wholly perished;
From mist to mist, we blink awhile:
A glass of wine or moment's laughter spent,
And each crawls out his scant Earth-measured mile.
But who upon a toy shall laugh,
Or who the good ale quaff,
Or who has told the unmalignant lie,
And not been Falstaff's debtor?
Indeed, Sir John, your mirth,
The world's whole store of roguish wit in one,
Still vibrant on the roofless tavern tops,
And ageless as at birth,
Serves us, plain wits, to sparkle for an hour
And mock Life's fretful shower,
Before the sexton tosses back the earth.
But, John, beware the Nordic prince who sits
Among the war-torn ruins,
Brooding yet,
Half in, half out his wits:

With one keen quip, imperishable Hamlet might
Snuff out your Devil's two-pronged light,
Turn mirth to honest tears,
And day to night would darken all our years.
Or will Macbeth, half shadowed by an alp,
Choose yours to Hamlet's scalp?

THE FRAYED CORD

Anchises, shrouded, stood once at the fore
Of richest gardens, near a gold-wrought door;
His bloodlines sprang most rich in ancient Rome
And died, I'm told, at New York's Hippodrome:
Just as the ersatz gods, white-wigged and hoar
    with age,
Bent from their upstairs stage,
And eyes were focused on the sawdust floor—
The act was billed as not performed before—
The lion scoffed to see Jove's firmament
Walled by a room as vulgar as a tent,
And blinked and chewed a mange-infected sore.
Mange-sick he died, but in an outdoor cage
And, dying, dreamed of jungles and, with pride,
Of legions mustered on the Tiber's side.
Bright noons, meantime, and Roman arches bore
A servile stamp—no balm to his heart's core.
Come, pass the brandy and the cheese-cake too;
There's one slight question I must ask of you:
Firm-willed the goshawk sped
Or, star-spent, lies he dead
On Caesar's ashes east of Labrador?

THE LONG WAIT

The bridge stands fair, and seems not hard to cross;
Beyond, the meadows to the mountains rise;
Fair springs, and autumns too,
Have gleamed, green-gold, against the blue.
Yet I sought neither spring's nor autumn's prize—
And winter peaks, much to my loss,
Mark where I should, but shall not cross.

The bridge stands fair, which spans the frozen stream,
And beckons, as it beckoned to my youth;
Indeed, I could still walk
Across that bridge and have my talk
And tell Life's Marshal what I can of truth.
But dare I say, "The stars will gleam
No brighter though I've crossed the stream"?

RAIN

No sorrow brings more wisdom than does rain
Which falls at night upon a window-pane.
In slow lament, it makes its plaintive song
As though it wept for twenty seasons long—
Forever weeping in a stark gray mood,
And rain alone accents the solitude,
Dark and opaque; oppressed at heart, we know
We are a dream shaped many years ago,
Self and not self. Remote and strange, we lie
And call to mind that self-same lullaby
Which, years ago, had made our young hearts sing:
Then, rain had talked of tulips and of spring.

DREAMFUL IS THE ROOT

Of all things dead there are sharp stirrings now;
For nothing dies and stays forever dead—
The day that sets, bird fallen from a bough,
The antelope age-sick on forest bed,
Or dolphin brooding in the last of dreams:
Whatever dies, again from dark root springs,
For Death is like a crystal light that gleams
Not on an end, but on immortal things.
The womb of Earth, and that of ocean too,
Wait on a dream of dreamful things to come;
Then why should we, when Death has come to woo,
Forget the pulse-beat and think of the tomb?
    Each shattered urn, spun in the womb of Earth,
    Holds promise, darkening, of a brightened birth.

OF BIRD AND WIND

Most folk have built stout walls and hold
    No kin-taught creed in doubt;
But I've been taught by ocean winds
    How much a wall shuts out.

Glad-eyed, I mark the scud of foam
    And find my heart's repose
In wind that comes from north and east
    And, thousand-throated, blows.

And when the hurricane has passed,
    I've yet to mount the shore;
For, most of all, my comfort lies
    In wind where white birds soar.

White bird and wind are envoys come
    From ocean's farthest tide:
They speak of drums and Zulu girls
    And gods who have not died.